Toucans

Victoria Blakemore

vblakemore.author@gmail.com

Copyright info/picture credits

Cover, Ondrej Prosicky/Shutterstock; Page 3, NatureFreak/Pixabay; Page 5, monikawl999/Pixabay; Page 7, WaSZI/Pixabay; Page 9, hanohiki/Adobestock; Pages 10-11, Fotos 593/AdobeStock; Page 13, reisegraf.ch/Shutterstock; Page 15, Brian Lasenby/AdobeStock; Page 17, dabldy/AdobeStock; Page 19, Chelsea Sampson/Shutterstock; Page 21, Vladimir Melnik/AdobeStock; Page 23; stefan/AdobeStock; Page 25, MicheleB/Shutterstock; Page 27, reisegraf/AdobeStock; Page 29, OneEarthCreations/Pixabay; Page 31, Pexels/Pixabay; Page 33, Ondrej Prosicky/Shutterstock

Table of Contents

What Are Toucans?

Toucans are a kind of bird that are found in tropical areas. They are known for their large bill and brightly colored feathers.

There are about forty different kinds of toucans. They differ in size, coloration, and where they are found in the wild.

Toucans have mostly black
feathers. They also have patches
of brightly colored feathers.

Size

Toucans **vary** in size. They can weigh anywhere from about three ounces to nearly two pounds.

The smallest toucan is the tawny-tufted toucanet. It can grow to be twelve inches tall. The largest is the toco toucan. It can grow to be twenty-four inches tall.

The green-billed toucan can weigh up to twelve ounces. It has a smaller beak than many toucans.

5

Physical Characteristics

Toucans have a very large, curved bill. Their bill helps them to pick fruit and build a nest in a tree trunk.

They have small wings for birds of their size. They can use them to fly short distances when needed. They are not good at flying very far.

Toucans have curved feet and sharp claws. This allows them to grasp branches as they move around the trees.

Habitat

Toucans are found in the rainforest. They spend most of their time high up in the canopy layer. It is very hot there.

Toucans can keep themselves cool with their large bill. They release **excess** heat through the many blood vessels in their bill.

Range

Toucans are only found in the wild in Central and South America.

They are often seen in countries such as Brazil, Panama, Bolivia, and Paraguay.

Diet

Most toucans are **frugivores**, which means that they eat only fruit. Some are **omnivores**. They eat meat and plants.

Most of their diet is made up of fruits such as figs, oranges, and guavas. Some also eat insects such as caterpillars or termites. Others sometimes eat bird eggs.

Toucans use their long bill to pick

fruit from trees.

Toucan bills have a **serrated** edge. They can use it to remove the skin from fruits before they eat them.

Toucans help their **ecosystem**. When they eat fruits, they swallow seeds. The seeds are spread throughout the rainforest through their **waste**. The seeds grow into new plants.

Toucans have a long, thin tongue. It is usually almost as long as their bill.

Communication

Toucans use mainly sound to communicate with each other. They are known for their loud, deep croaking sounds that can be heard from far away.

They have a rattling call that they often use. They also make a loud clacking sound with their bill.

Toucans have a special call they use if a predator is near. It warns other toucans of the danger.

Movement

Like most birds, toucans can
fly. However, their small wings
make it hard for them. They
are not very good at flying.

When they do fly, they flap
their wings fast and glide on
the air. They can only fly for
short distances at a time.

Toucans usually move from tree to tree by hopping along the branches.

Toucan Chicks

Toucans lay between one and five eggs. The male and female toucans take turns sitting on the eggs. It can take up to eighteen days for them to hatch.

When the chicks hatch, they are blind and do not have feathers. Their feathers start to grow in after about three weeks.

Toucan chicks are ready to leave the nest for the first time after between six and eight weeks.

Toucan Life

Toucans are very social birds. They live in groups that are called flocks. Each flock can have up to about twenty toucans.

Flocks work together to watch for **predators**. They also play-fight with their large bills.

Toucans can travel very far each day looking for food. They travel mainly by hopping from tree to tree.

Nests

Toucans make their nests inside of tree trunks. To make their nest, they use their large bill to peck a hole.

Once the hole is just large enough to fit their body, they can climb inside. Toucans have to curl their body up to fit into their small nests.

Toucans sleep in their nests at

night. They also lay their eggs

there.

Population

Most toucans are not currently **endangered**. However, many populations are **declining** in the wild.

The yellow-browed toucanet is currently **endangered**. There are not many left in the wild. It could become **extinct**.

It is not known how long toucans

live in the wild. In zoos, many live

up to eighteen years.

Toucans in Danger

Toucans are facing several threats from people. The main threat is habitat loss. Toucan habitats are being cut down for buildings, roads, and farmland.

In some places, toucans are hunted. Some are hunted for **sport**. Others are caught to be sold.

Wild toucans are often taken

from their habitat to be sold as

pets.

Helping Toucans

Many groups are trying to help toucans. Some focus on saving their rainforest habitat. They want to protect the rainforest so that animals like toucans have a safe habitat to live in.

Some countries have laws against hunting toucans for **sport**.

Places like the Toucan Rescue Ranch help toucans that are sick or hurt. They take care of them until they can be released back into the wild.

Other groups focus on research and education. They want to learn more about toucans in the wild so they can help them.

Glossary

Declining: getting smaller

Ecosystem: living things and the habitat they live in

Endangered: at risk of becoming extinct

Excess: extra

Extinct: when there are no more of an animal left in the wild

Frugivore: animals that eat only fruit

Omnivore: an animal that eats meat and plants

Predator: an animal that hunts other animals for food

Serrated: having a grooved edge, like a saw

Sport: when animals are hunted for fun, not for food

Vary: differ

Waste: material given off by the body after food is digested

About the Author

Victoria Blakemore is a first grade

teacher in Southwest Florida with a

passion for reading.

You can visit her at

www.elementaryexplorers.com

Also in This Series

Gray Wolves · Sloths · Flamingos · Camels · Koalas · Honey Bees · Pandas · Pangolins

White-Tailed Deer · Orcas · Giraffes · Corn · Meerkats · Echidnas · Walruses · Raccoons

Bald Eagles · Apples · Arctic Foxes · Red Pandas · Cassowaries · Tigers · Ladybugs · Moose

Beluga Whales · Leopards · Elephants · Jellyfish · Binturongs · Lions · Dolphins · Reindeer

Hammerhead Sharks · Hippos · Pumpkins · Peafowl · Chameleons · Florida Panthers · Aye-Ayes · Black Bears

Cheetahs · Manatees · Gingerbread · Polar Bears · Hot Chocolate · Orangutans · Coyotes · Marshmallows

Strawberries · Aardvarks · Mako Sharks · Alligators · Frogs · Hedgehogs · Brown Bears · Bongos

Sea Turtles · Quokkas · Muskrats · Zebras · Red Foxes · Ring-Tailed Lemurs · Platypuses · Anteaters

Also in This Series

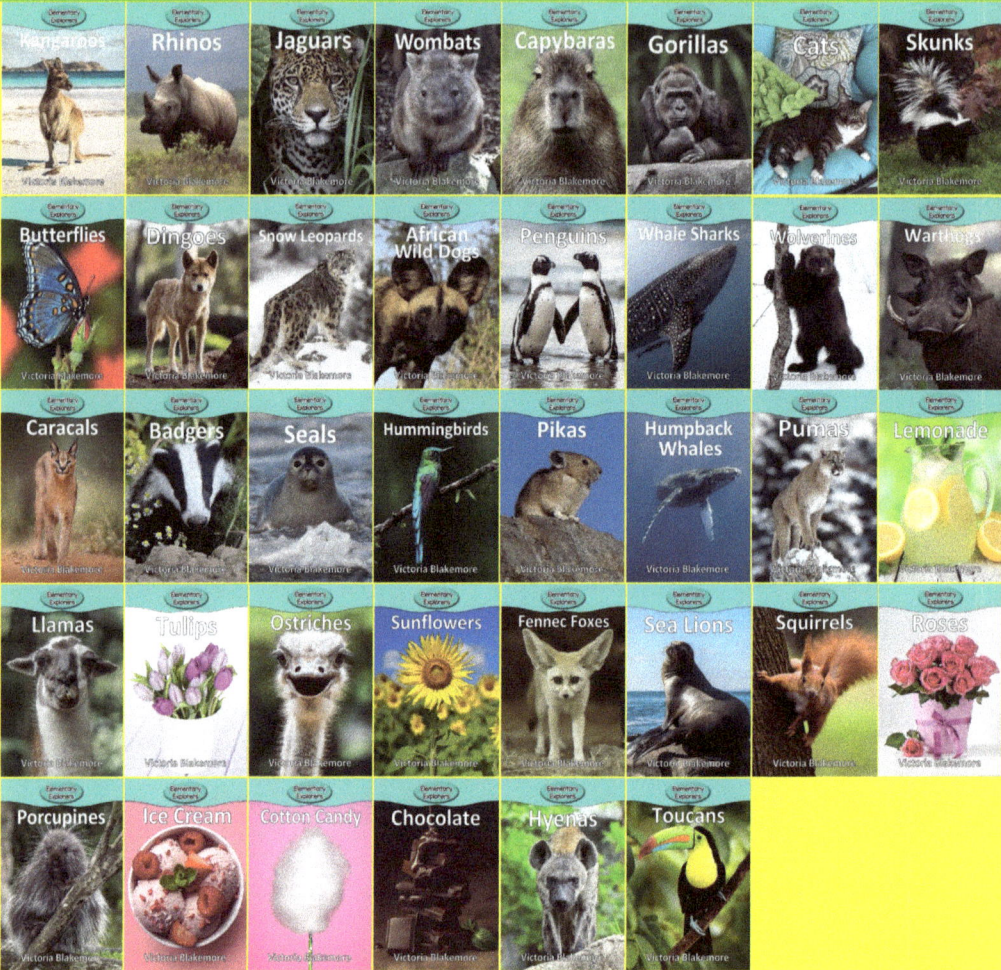

Kangaroos	Rhinos	Jaguars	Wombats	Capybaras	Gorillas	Cats	Skunks
Butterflies	Dingoes	Snow Leopards	African Wild Dogs	Penguins	Whale Sharks	Wolverines	Warthogs
Caracals	Badgers	Seals	Hummingbirds	Pikas	Humpback Whales	Pumas	Lemonade
Llamas	Tulips	Ostriches	Sunflowers	Fennec Foxes	Sea Lions	Squirrels	Roses
Porcupines	Ice Cream	Cotton Candy	Chocolate	Hyenas	Toucans		

Victoria Blakemore

www.ingramcontent.com/pod-product-compliance
Lightning Source LLC
Chambersburg PA
CBHW051254020426
42333CB00025B/3204